Learning to Live, Laugh, And Love Again

After the Death of an Adult Child

By
Jan Jaworski

w/am

Thank you for your

friendship Jan

XULON PRESS

Table of Contents

Introduction

✿ ✿

I lost my daughter!

If you saw me today, you would never suspect that I have buried my daughter. It has been more than five years since I last saw Karen, yet she is never far from my thoughts. Today she is always with me in my life, only you do not know it. I was fortunate to have had Karen grace my life for 31 years.

How did I let her go when the doctors said it was time to remove her life support because she was losing her battle with cancer? How have I learned to incorporate her death into my life? How have I learned to live without her in my life? How has my marriage of 33 years survived? How have I faced other obstacles in my life, such as caring for my elderly mother? I felt I had no choice but to rebuild my life. I still had a husband and a son who need me.

The apple cart of my wonderful midlife years was turned upside down and inside out when I lost my daughter to cancer. It pulled my husband, my son and me together in ways we never imagined as we helped Karen fight for her life. How do we go on as a family with a member no longer in our presence? I never imagined that I would ever write this book. Am I really doing this? Am I still living some dream, some cruel nightmare?

Many times in my grief journey, I told my psychologist, Donn Peters, that I could not find a book that described my feelings. I scoured the book-stores looking for such a book. I wanted to read about my grief from a mother who had lost her adult child so I could relate to her.

Then Donn suggested I write the book that I had been looking for. My husband, Ken, immediately joined my support team, along with a host of friends who encouraged me to write about my experiences in my healing journey.

The hard reality is that I am not dreaming. My loss is real. My precious daughter is gone. And now I am typing at the computer, telling you about it not to only aid my own healing, but to assist you with yours. Together we will cry, we will mourn, but ulti-mately we will heal.

Please join me as I share my trials and joys with you. Life does go on after losing a child. If I can do it, so can you. Hold my hand now, as I hold yours. Cry on my shoulder as I cry on yours. I am here for you. Be there for me.

Chapter 1.

In death there are lessons to be learned

It has been five years since Karen died

It was one of those delightful spring evenings, when good friends get together for dinner. My husband, Ken, and I stood looking out our living room window watching Jane and Jack drive down our steep hill heading back to Salt Lake City. The mountain sky was filled with stars.

As I stood at the window I remarked to my husband Ken about the relaxing evening we had spent with our dear friends. I had planned it that way. I wanted it to be old friends catching up on each others lives in a relaxing low key evening. Since we had moved to Park City about a year ago we didn't see Jane and Jack nearly as much as we had when we lived in the Salt Lake City area. So all of us treasured the time we now spent together. The evening had been filled with warmth and caring. And yet something was missing.

As I wiped a tear from my eye I gently said to Ken, "No one said a word about Karen". I had thought of her throughout the evening and at one point mid way through dinner I nearly said, "This is the fifth anniversary of her death." Then I thought to myself, "No, I don't want to ruin our evening."

Ken and I stood looking out at the stars wondering where in the heavens Karen was. Was Karen up on this or that star? I said to Ken, "I have come a long way; we both have in the past five years. It is hard to believe we now live in the town Karen loved so much. The past five years haven't been easy, but we have survived. Yes, I am getting better." As I reflected in my mind, I knew I'd handled myself exceptionally well this evening.

The garden path

Several years ago Jane and I went to a local home show at a Convention Center. As we walked around, we came to a booth with landscapes done in oil. I rummaged through them, and one painting really caught my eye.

The unframed painting done in soft muted pastel oils, showed flowers in yellow and shades of pink reminding me of wild roses. I thought of these flowers surrounded by lush green vegetation. A pathway wondered through the middle of it, and ended with a gate. The wrought iron gate set in the tall stone wall. The gate was swung partially open. Through the gate you could see tall trees beyond. This painting just grabbed my heart and soul.

Jane and I continued to wander around the home show looking at all the exhibits, and gathering decorating ideas. We were having a wonderful day out, but my mind kept wandering back to that painting with the garden gate. I couldn't get the picture out of my mind. I love Thomas Kinkaid's paintings of landscapes, and this picture reminded me of his work without the price tag.

When Jane and I reached the end of the displays I said, "I want to go back to the booth with the oil paintings." I shared with her how I loved the painting, and then I bought it. Today the painting is beautifully framed and hangs in my home. I have a garden bench in front of it in an entry area.

The painting reminds me daily of the path Karen and I once walked down. I could only go so far. I had to let my beautiful daughter continue down through the gate by her self as she continued her pathway to heaven. As painful as it was to see her go, I could not follow. I know someday, I will walk down that pathway, meet her again and hold her forever.

So in the meantime I am reminded of how I had to let Karen go.

The beginning of the end

Karen came into this world a little late as I carried her ten months. She was worth the wait and was perfect in every way. She was full of life from the moment she arrived. Karen loved to sing and dance.

She embraced life for all it had to offer. She had the type of personality that made in immediate impression on you as someone you wanted to get to know better. Karen cared about you as a person. She was warm and caring. She would do anything for you. Karen loved nature. I envied her green thumb she could bring a near dead plant back to life with her magical touch. She loved to go to the farmers market. I can just picture her with her straw summer hat on, with her long wavy brown hair flowing beneath it as she shopped.

We moved to Sandy, Utah, at the south end of the Salt Lake Valley when Karen was in junior high school. When Karen was 28 years old, in 1998, she decided to move about 30 miles away to Park City, Utah, where she worked in the tourist industry, and enjoyed all this picturesque little town had to offer. Karen could go cross country skiing in the morning before going to work in the afternoon. She was happy and single. She made friends easily and kept an eye out for Mr. Right to come into her life. She dreamed of one day buying a condo of her own.

In the fall of 2000 at age 30, Karen was diagnosed with TMJ (Temporomandibular Joint Syndrome) a disorder that produces pain and stiffness of the joint between the lower jawbone, and the temporal bone of the skull. A simple name for it is lockjaw. She immediately began treatment. In February, 2001, Karen started losing the use of her left eye. By now the pain in her jaw was so great she decided it was time for surgery to rebuild her jaw. In late February, Karen had both jaw joints rebuilt in surgery to correct the

TMJ. We wondered if a nerve linked to the painful jaw was affecting her eye.

Two weeks after the surgery, Karen had severe chest pains, and her friend Sue took her to the emergency clinic in Park City. Ken and I were called at our home in nearby Sandy, and asked to come to the clinic. Karen needed us!

The doctors suspected there was more to this story as they examined Karen. Karen was transferred a short time later to the Emergency Room at the University of Utah Medical Center. The chest pains had stopped, but the doctors wanted to do further tests on Karen. Karen's left eye was now forced shut, and we all wondered why? We were now on pins and needles, as we waited for more information!

Within a few short hours Karen was diagnosed with cancer which began in her left sinus. She began treatments to stop it from spreading. In a few weeks, they gave us the complete name of the rare type of cancer. Karen had: spindle cell rhabdomyosarcoma cancer, derived from muscle cells angioplasty which are very aggressive and rapid growing. We were about to learn this was one mean, angry cancer that spreads quickly through the body.

The fight of our lives had begun. Our son, Brian, a year younger than Karen, returned to Utah to help and comfort his sister, and us. We were all in total shock. Karen was put on prayer chains around the country.

The cancer raged with a vengeance like a wild-fire through Karen's body. She was upbeat and optimistic as she followed the doctor's orders. Karen always wanted to know up front about her condition. She listened to doctors and made her own decisions regarding her treatments. Karen was in and out of the hospital several times. She was too weak to return to her apartment and so she stayed with Ken, Brian and I. Managing her health care required 24 hours a day supervision.

We did have good family times as we made family dinners together in our large kitchen, and played board games together. We shared many stories about our life's adventures. Brian has traveled to the far ends of the world, while Karen had explored the intermountain west. Ken and I loved to hear their stories about their travels. We also talked about those family camping trips of long ago and the camping trips we looked forward to taking when Karen was well enough.

The four of us went to our church on Easter Sunday. Ken and I later took Karen to see my mother, Melba, for a brief visit at her assisted living complex. This would be our last public outing with Karen.

Karen went into the hospital a few days after Easter to begin a two day chemo treatment. She had to first have blood platelet infusions to make her blood healthy enough to receive the chemo.

Six weeks into her cancer diagnosis Karen could no longer breathe on her own. She was still in the hospital having her chemo treatment. She was told of her critical condition and she made the decision to go on life support hoping to buy time for the chemo and radiation treatments to work. Even gaining one extra week could be all it took.

Several days later the doctors called our family to a special meeting. Karen was dying! We were told she only had days, perhaps only hours to live.

Dr. Lund volunteered to be the one to tell Karen.

Words can't describe how we felt! I felt as if my life ended when I heard those words "Karen is dying". (In a way, it did that day.) Oh, how I wanted to trade places with her! As I sat in the ICU Conference Room, I asked Dr. Lund to show me on the computer where the cancer was located in Karen's body. He gently explained it all to Ken, Brian and me. Karen's lungs were gone; one was folded over. Both were surrounded by a cancer mass. The cancer was in her intestines and liver. The tumor in her sinus was the size of a can of soda pop putting pressure on her brain. I just wanted to scream: Not my daughter!!!!!! "No, this has to be some nightmare!! I wanted to wake up.

Now we were all in shock! We only had a brief time remaining with Karen.

Dr. Lund told Karen that the cancer had won! She was soooo brave as she took the news pending death. Now all we could do was to make her as comfortable as possible and let nature take its course. All I could do was hold her hand and tell her how much I loved her.

We treasured every moment we spent with Karen, and we all prayed for her peaceful passing.

The following day she wrote her final requests on a sheet of paper. Ken, Brian and I all said our "good byes" to Karen, each in our own way.

The doctors advised us that it was time to remove the life support. Karen's pain was out of control and could no longer be mellowed with medication. The cancer had consumed her body. There was no hope of recovery. It was the loving thing to do.

Seven short weeks after we had arrived at the Emergency Room, we were now in the ICU unit, saying our final "I love you's" to Karen.

Ken held her left hand while I held her right hand. Karen let go of my hand to wave. Was it "good bye" to us or "hello to Jesus?" Karen's spirit was gone.

Karen died on Sunday, April 29, 2001. She was 31 years old.

The wrath of Karen's cancer was brief

Many concerned people came to me after Karen died to tell me, "Be glad she didn't suffer too long." Karen enjoyed life each day. She never considered death as an option in her fight against cancer. Yes, we did have many quality family times during her illness. Karen did survive cancer for 49 days. That is something to be proud of!

Jane and Jack came to dinner

I believe the gift of friendship is one of the greatest gifts we can give. One could never ask for more dedicated friends than Jane and Jack. They were at our side in the Emergency Room the day Karen was diagnosed with cancer. Throughout her illness they were always in close contact with us, never more than a telephone call away, regardless of the time of day.

Jane knew I had a long night at the hospital. She appeared on the morning of Karen being put on life support with a bag for me to freshen up with. She knew just what I needed: a toothbrush, toothpaste and a washcloth along with some perfume, but more than that I needed her.

It was natural for Jane and Jack to want us to come to dinner at their house the night Karen died, but I wanted to be at home. So they came to us knowing that we didn't have any family in the area. Instead they had become our adopted family over the years. They too had lost someone very special in their lives, our daughter.

True friends can weather out our storms. Now a new storm was brewing in our lives only we had a few more items of new business to finish up.

Karen's final wishes

Karen gave us one last gift when she wrote out her final wishes. She knew that we would honor them by our love for her. We cremated her as she requested. Then we held a celebration of her life at her church in Park City, and we buried her in an unmarked grave in a location she had requested.

I believe we were on auto pilot as we carried out her wishes, and went through the motions of honoring her life. I thought at the time I was working with a sound mind, but, in reality, I was only going through the motions of living.

Now we must remember Karen had left her apartment with every intention of returning. It became our labor of love and discovery to dismantle her apartment. Karen had several more surprises up her sleeve. Ken, Brian and I each learned more about the type of person Karen was, and we learned what was really important to her. She was an avid reader; she had over 500 books on a huge array of subjects. While she seldom used her television it was buried in a closet. She was saving it to watch the 2002 Winter Olympics to be held in Park City.

In one closet I found all the dresses that were important to her. I found formals from her high school dances. There was the dark rose red, off the shoulder dress she wore to a fall dance with its long flowing skirt. She had her picture taken with her date at the dance. Then there was the spring formal dance when she wore a yellow dress with an over lay of white eyelet. It too was an off the shoulder dress, and again she had her picture taken with her date. In the pictures from dance you can see the swim suit top tan lines. The dress she wore under her cap and gown to her college graduation was a flowered summer dress with lace trim. As was her style she always wore her long brown wavy hair down as it brought out the color of her brown eyes. She was the smallest person in her graduation class at five foot one inch. She stands out in the pictures because of her size. Her face dances with joy in all of her pictures.

In one closet I discovered a real treasure. Karen had almost completed a cross stitch of the poem

Bless This House. Today this poem hangs framed in a hallway of our home just as she left it.

Karen does Bless This House, but more importantly God Blesses This House!

Accepting words of sympathy

I am the first to say I have a hard time accepting someone trying to convey sympathy to me. I want to freeze in place. I don't know how to react to people when they want to give me a hug or make nice comments of affection and express their concern to me. I was raised in a house where hugging was not done. Over the years I have learned to accept and give hugs to people who are special friends in my life. I have never been good at taking a compliment. I want to brush them off. Now I knew that with Karen's death this wasn't possible. I suddenly realized my learning curve of life was about to change. I had a fast advance course in accepting genuine caring. I had experienced every parent's worst nightmare. I had met NEVER my child had died. A parent NEVER dreams of having a child die.

I realized no matter how uneasy I was personally I had to learn to put people at ease. I learned how to relax. I had been at a loss for words myself when I have been to funerals for friends who have lost their child. Now it was my turn to be on the receiving end. Yes, I had to remind myself it is the thought that counts, not necessarily the words.

Believe me I heard some strange comments like, "She was so young". While I am thinking that, yes,

I know she was too young to die, I am her mother! I realized from the first day that there would be times when I had to turn the negative into the positive in my mind for the sympathizer.

I knew one thing for sure. I was now on unfamiliar ground in my life. Now that I had made it past the memorial and dismantling of Karen's apartment, how would I go on with my life now? I felt like I was going into an uncharted sea. I was lost at sea without a compass.

A whole new world was about to open up to me. I was going to learn about death in a very personal way.

Chapter 2.

Death is a difficult word to learn

Death was a difficult word for me to add to my everyday vocabulary. I found it so hard to say, "My daughter is dead." I found some people just didn't understand it when I said, "My daughter has passed away." I guess they didn't think that our children die. There was a time or two that I said, "My daughter is in heaven." This really threw people for a loop. They would say, "What?" Then I was back to, "She died." We are born then we die. Sometimes the circle of life is completed way too soon. Karen died too soon. Now I found it so painful to say she is dead.

A new journey has begun

I was lost in my early grief. Then one day, I started using the word "journey" to describe life without Karen. For so many years, Karen's life had been a road on my map of life. At her death, that road came to a dead end on the map, and so did I. Now, I would have to find a new way to continue on my journey without her. The map of my life was changed forever.

Grief has often been described as similar to losing a body part through amputation. I felt like I had a huge hole in my heart, as if part of it had been forcefully removed without anesthesia. The pain was unimaginable. I knew I could never replace Karen. Now I would have to find how to chart my life from here on out. This new journey through life wouldn't be easy but it could be done.

I choose to get out of bed each day

Some grieving mothers pull the covers over their heads for months, rarely going beyond the front door. I am an active person, and I had responsibilities demanding my attention.

In the days following Karen's death, I decided to get out of bed. Some mornings, it was hard, yet my inner voice said, "It is time to get up and face the day, Jan." So I made myself think about what I wanted to accomplish that day, and I was grateful for my warm house and the soft carpet I would feel as I got out of bed. I was grateful that my life was comfortable.

It takes courage to get out of bed when we are hurting. But there is this little voice inside my soul that says, "There is something special for you today. Get up and go find it." When I got out of bed, in those early days after Karen's death, I'd go right away to look out the window, to see what was new in my world. Karen died in the spring, a time of new life outdoors, so I would check to see what new flowers had bloomed. I wanted to see that I had a new life ahead of me.

I knew I had a choice. As much as I wanted to scream, "Stop the world, my daughter has just died!" I couldn't. I did stumble around for a time, not sure if I wanted to be part of the human race and greet each day with a positive outlook. But I soon realized that even though Karen had lost her life, I hadn't lost mine.

I began to realize that life had presented me with a new journey. One day, I found a stone sculpture for the front yard that said exactly what I was coming to realize: "Life is a journey, enjoy the ride." I could choose to sit on the sidelines of life, or I could choose to enjoy the ride, no matter how difficult it was. The choice was mine. I chose to live my life as a new journey unfolding every day, even as I grieved Karen.

Each day will have challenges

Life is not fair. This is simple to see. I had hit a sharp, unexpected curve in my life. There were some days that I had to rethink everything I was doing. Some days even the easiest task became so hard to do. I had to remind myself to go easy on myself and lower my expectations and then my life ran smoother.

In my grief, I wanted easy solutions to everyday problems. Many days I had to stand back and think to myself, "Is there another way around this problem, some days this took more thought than others. But what counted was the end result.

I found that in my grief, all of my emotions were raw, as if I had been stripped down to my raw nerves. At times, I felt like I was bleeding grief in every aspect of my life. Sometimes I could cover my emotions with small talk. Other times, I didn't care about bothering.

My new learning curve about life

Now I faced a new challenge. I had survived the harshest unexpected hairpin turn of my life. I knew whatever I would now face would never be as severe as Karen's death. But I wondered if I could handle any curves at all.

The answer came to me when I thought about how I drive my little sports car in the summer; I love driving it on roads with long, sweeping curves, but I'm cautious—-you never know when you'll come upon a tight turn. I have learned to go into the turn slowly and accelerate as I exit the turn. It occurred to me that this approach applied to my life. When something unexpected comes along, go in slowly. Then get the feel of the road and accelerate when it feels comfortable to do so.

I have also learned that when I drive my SUV during the winter months, I can't take the turns as fast as I do in my sports car. I believe each experience in life is a little different. I realized that I would learn as I go how to handle the curves.

I once saw a license plate that said "YGROWUP". I agree! I sometime wish I didn't have to grow up. I decided for myself that this was one of those times in life when we have to grow up and face the life we have been given, for better or worse.

My heart is broken

My broken heart will not be mended. I remember, as a little girl, walking across the living room with a boysenberry pie in my hands. I suddenly tripped and fell, and the pie went flying all over my mother's new rug. As hard as I scrubbed, I could always see some of the stain in that rug for as long as she owned it. Grief is like a permanent stain that will always be on our hearts. It is up to us to decide if we choose to focus on the stain left by our grief, or if we want to concentrate on the beauty of the life around us.

Obviously, we can't go out and get a new child to replace the one we have lost. But I believe there is another way to mend our lives. My mother used to knit a lot when I was a child. I'd often watch her use her knitting needles to cover a mistake that she had made, making it look good like there had never been a mistake in the first place. We don't always have to let our flaws show. We can cover our emotions when we need to protect ourselves; we can learn to cover our pain when we need to protect our emotions. My mother used her knitting needles to cover the flaws in the garment she was making. In grief, we can learn to knit new relationships. We can reach out to the children around us as we celebrate their lives, and we continue to knit our own lives.

I have asthma, and have had to learn how to adjust to it. Just like my asthma, I decided I had to incorporate Karen's death into my life. And as with my asthma, I know the triggers of my grief that will set off my mood swings or a flood of tears. It is now up to me to learn to control them. Early on in my grief, I made it a long-term goal to learn to incorporate my grief into my life so that others wouldn't know that I was a grieving mother unless I told them so. As her mother, it is my story to tell. It is just like my asthma; who do I want to tell about it?

My physical and mental self

I was advised early in my grief to have my health supervised by a physician the first year or so, to keep an eye on my asthma and general health. Grief is hard work! It drains a huge amount of strength from our bodies. Over the years, I have found that when I monitor my grief with a physician on a regular basis, I perform much better in life.

In my grief, my immune system was also very low. I was more susceptible to colds and any bug that was going around at the time. I have learned over the years to protect myself. I am not afraid to get up at a movie theater and change seats if someone is coughing and sneezing around me.

I also have to watch the calorie intake. I love chocolate, but too much can increase my weight. I don't want to have to work harder later on to take it off. I am the first to admit that I do not like scales. I can tell by how my clothes fit if I need to cut my portions in half. We each live in our own bodies and it is up to us to learn how to protect ourselves.

I learned through trial and error that I had to look after myself so I could be healthy for my family. I found when I lowered my expectations of what I can and can't do my days of multitasking were gone. Suddenly everything in life got so much easier. Grief is hard work—it drains you physically and mentally. So when I looked after myself, I knew I was healthier mentally and physically.

I learned to take a big task, such as cleaning out the kitchen cupboards, and break it down into much smaller task so I could get the job done. I would clean one drawer or two at a time, and then before long the entire kitchen was cleaned. This example is one that reminds me to break a large task down into smaller, more manageable tasks I can get the job done.

I don't like clutter around the house. I find there are small things I can do to unclutter my mind. When my closets are tidy and clean I perform much better in my life. Somehow cleaning also clears up the clutter in my mind. We all have little idiosyncrasies in our lives. Sometimes we just need to take personal time to address them, which puts our minds in a better place.

In coping with my grief, I remind myself that I have to take baby steps before I can run. As I walk on unfamiliar ground, there are days when I have to slow my pace down and stay focused on where I am going. Looking to the past only reminds me of the pain and loss I feel. When I look from side to side, I am reminded that life goes on all around me. When we lived in England, I remember walking on cobblestone walkways. I had to walk carefully to keep my balance on the rounded stones. Now my grief reminds me of those rounded stones. Soon the path ahead will level itself out, and I can walk with ease again, as I move forward on my new journey.

Self-esteem was another area I had to work on after Karen's death. I felt like a popped balloon discarded after a party. I was at the lowest point of my life, internally and externally. One day I looked in the mirror and decided I deserved to work on my outside. I had let my hair return to its natural mousy brown. This had to go. So I called the beauty salon, made an appointment, and got a new look. Then, I remembered years ago, I had enjoyed massages, so I got a massage. My body needed this extra attention to let go of the stress that I carried. Over the years, this has become one of my indulgences. When I feel better on the inside, it shows on the outside, and helps me improve my outlook on life. This is another way of being healthy for the world around me.

I have another yard art stone that says, "The world laughs in flowers." I find a lot of truth in that phase. I can choose to be a folded up flower, refusing to bloom, or I can let my life unfold like a flower. I want to bloom and grow like a flower but in my grief this is very hard. I also need to recognize when I have made a mistake so I can turn my mistake into laughter. I had to learn to laugh again, in particular, at myself I forgot that I am human after all. Some days I think there is a fine line between laughing and crying. Which would you rather I do?

We all carry some form of baggage in life. All we need to do is to stop and look around us. I decided to watch my friends and see how they carried their personal baggage so I could learn from them.

Then I thought about Ken and Brian. How were they carrying the baggage of Karen's death?

Speaking of others, it is about time to talk about my family. Oh, there are so many lessons to be learned from them.

Chapter 3.

The needs of my family

As a child, I lived near my grandparents. Over the years, I've gathered wonderful memories, of my aunts, uncles and cousins coming and going as they visited from out of town. Today, these memories are part of the framework of my childhood. Each person had a role in my life and in enriching my childhood.

As an adult, my life branched out and I created a new family frame with my family. Some extended relatives appeared briefly after Karen's death. Most of my relatives have drifted back into my life if only for a brief time. I did appreciate it when some of them called from time to time to check on me. I do not think they understood the gravity of our loss. How could they?

When Karen became ill, we called Ken's sister, Mary, to share the terrible news, and stayed in weekly contact for those seven weeks. So we were shocked and hurt when Mary told us she couldn't come to

Karen's memorial because she had to attend a real estate seminar. Several months later, I told her how hurt I was that she did not attend. I handled the situation with the diplomacy of a bull in a china shop. My remarks to her started a rift between us that would last almost five years. Then one Christmas I decided to send her a Christmas card. To my surprise, she answered it right away. Today, we correspond now and then via email. To this day, I wonder if Mary will ever tell us the truth why she did not attend Karen's memorial. But does it matter?

All of these people have played a part in my in life. Now, only a few will continue to be close to me. What is important for me to remember is that they have helped me to build character so I can find the strength to go on without Karen.

Brian continues his education. Hurray!

Our son, Brian, is eighteen months younger than Karen. He has always been an independent person. He has traveled the world as a career missionary with Mercy Ships. He came home to Utah to support his sister with her cancer battle. Two weeks after her death, he returned to Mercy Ships International Office in Texas. This is where he would mourn his sister.

As adults, Brian and Karen always remained close. He spent many hours by her side in the final weeks of her life. They had laughed, joked, and shared stories of their life experiences. During the quiet times as she lay in the hospital bed, he read the Bible to her.

I have always prayed for the safety and well-being of my children. I knew in my heart that Brian could look after himself, but with Karen's death so fresh in my mind, I worried about him incessantly. I wanted desperately to protect Brian. Brian asked Karen's doctors if there was a chance he would develop the same type of cancer that had claimed Karen's life. We were all relieved to discover there was not a genetic connection.

My parents decided when I was a child they would only have one child. I was aware of the responsibility of being an only child. Now Brian was the surviving child, though he could never be the only child. All the same, suddenly his role in the dynamics of our family had changed. Now I know first hand the responsibilities Brian would face sooner or later as Ken and I went from middle age to senior citizens. Someday Brian would be responsible for our elder care. I wanted to make this new awareness pain free for Brian. Ken and I decided that after 30 years it was time to update our wills and powers of attorney, so we did.

Now, with Brian out of state, I tried not to worry about him. He was great about calling home several times a week. What I had not counted on was how Brian would worry about Ken and me. The worry gene runs both ways in a family!

I tried to convince myself that worrying was only a waste of time. Slowly over time, worrying became less important to me. This is growth in the grieving process when we recognize a trait and slowly get it under control in our minds. This is not to say I do not worry, but I am more selective on what I worry about.

As Brian mourned Karen, he thought about what he wanted to accomplish in his life. We were thrilled and stunned when we got a telephone call from him saying, "I have decided to return to college at the University of Texas." Did we hear right? This was Brian's third go around at college. We were amazed at how he buckled down and took 18 units most semesters. Two years later Ken and I drove to Tyler, Texas, to attend Brian's college graduation. At dinner after the graduation, I asked Brian if Karen had anything to do with his decision to return to college. He told us that Karen had encouraged him when he was down by saying you can do it!

For many years, friends had always asked if Brian would go to seminary to become a pastor. I often replied that is was up to him. In Brian's final semester of college, he decided it was time to try seminary.

Ken and I were delighted when he decided to move back to Salt Lake City to attend Salt Lake Theological Seminary to earn a master's degree. Today, Brian is single, living and working in Salt Lake City. He is taking a break from his studies, but we know when the time is right he will return to the seminary.

Today, we see Brian quite often. He comes to our new house in Park City. He and Pepper, our chocolate Labrador, hike on the trails around our neighborhood.

One day I asked Brian to share a Karen memory with me. He shared how Karen saw and encouraged him to use his artistic abilities. Today he uses that talent through the lens of his camera.

I have always believed that as a parent it was my job to give my children a good foundation in life. Then as adults, I would watch them build on that foundation, as they became the person that God wanted them to become. I am proud of Brian today.

Now I am the caregiver for my elderly mother

My mother and I have always had a strained relationship. She was never close to me as a child or an adult. She was never a warm fuzzy type of person who I could feel close to being around. It was not in her personality; and instead she was always somewhat distant with me. I had always dreaded the day when I might have to take over her care in her declining years. That day came when she fell in her home and lay on the floor for 36 to 40 hours until she was found by the gardener. I was on the next airplane to San Diego.

We moved my 85-year-old mother, Melba, from her home of 51 years in San Diego, in January 2001, just two months before Karen was diagnosed with cancer. To put it simply, Mom and eldercare did not come with an owner's manual, or if they did, I did not have time to read it. So at the time of Karen's cancer, Mom was settling into her new home at an assisted living complex. I had several friends who visited her while Karen was ill. I tried to go see her at least once a week.

Then the bottom of my life fell out, when Karen was gone. Mom and Karen had been the best of friends. Mom saw me as an intruder in their relationship. Suddenly I wondered why I had lost my 31-year-old daughter and inherited my 85-year-old mother. Why had Mom survived a fall five months before? Was God trying to tell me something?

Mom had always been a very independent woman. She was an identical twin, and did not have the opportunity to become her own person until her college years in the late 1930's. She had raised me to be an independent person, also. Now she would show her independence again to me. Mom refused to be emotionally present for me as I grieved the loss of my daughter. I was heart broken.

So now, I had another huge problem on my shoulders. How do I continue to be my mother's caregiver and protect myself? I thought long and hard about it. Then I decided that I would do everything in my power to make sure my mother had the dignity and life style that she wanted for the remainder of her life. In the years to come, my new theory would be put to the test from time to time. Growing old is not for sissies. Eldercare is not for the weak.

My 90-pound mother lived life her own way for the next two-and-a-half years. I stepped in when the assisted living complex called me with a problem. Then one day it was time for her to go into a hospice facility. As nature took its course with her, I never gave up hope of connecting with her. Mom had always loved Ken. When the three of us were together, she didn't see me. Now as her final days approached, I still tried to get her attention but to no avail.

Finally one day, as her body was shutting down, she told me that she loved me. This was an unexpected gift from her. She had gone without food for over a week, when I asked one of her nurses if I could give her some ice cream. I will never forget the look on her face as I spoon-fed her ice cream. Her face lit up the room with pleasure. This was my parting gift to her and it ended her life on a high note for me.

Several days later on April 1, 2004, mom died. She was 88 years old. We held off scattering her ashes seven weeks until Brian graduated from college. On a bright sunny day, Ken, Brian and I, along with some family friends, took Mom for one last sail. We turned the boat into the wind and let the sails flap as I scattered Mom's ashes. We threw fresh flowers into the ocean that became a colorful tribute, rising and falling with the waves. On our way back into the harbor, we sailed past her beloved yacht club, ending a long life with a celebration she would have wanted to attend.

Our family members may put us to a test many times and when they do, we need to stop and think how would I want to be treated? As I reflect back on my mother's life, I remember all of the positive and negative lessons that she taught me. They all added to my growth as a human being.

Ken and I after 33 years of marriage, now what

Ken and I had been married two years when Karen was born, and Brian arrived eighteen months later. We thought we were mature adults when we married. We were both 20 years old—too young to drink or vote. Oh, we said we'd love until death do us part, but even after the death of a child? There had been nothing in my marriage vows about that.

We are learning new things about each other in grief

Ken and I each are strong willed. Suddenly when we were facing the loss of our daughter's life, survival was up for grabs. Many a day we were on a collision course. I'm sure the neighbors heard the sparks fly more than once. We can be like oil and water, and yet somehow we manage to function together. Our strength was what allowed us to survive.

Many days Ken and I were on very different playing fields. He dealt with grief as though he were a hockey player, skating through life padded to shield him from sadness, and ice cold to my needs; while I was a tennis player, out there rushing around exposing myself to everything and pounding him with volley after volley.

I still had so much to learn about Ken, or was it because I had to learn about myself as I continued on this grief journey?

Men and women grieve differently

Men grieve differently from women. I've heard this hundreds of times in my grief journey, but I did not want to believe it. I was off in my own world of pain, and I wanted Ken to join me there. After all, we were Karen's parents—shouldn't we grieve her death together in the same way? I thought that after 33 years of marriage, he should know what I was thinking. Wrong! I didn't understand why Ken could not be there for me the way I imagined he should.

I had had a very special connection to Karen. After all, I had carried her for ten months. Ken had only watched my pregnancy. I began to think my pain was greater than Ken's! I forgot to give Ken credit for having a part in her creation. We had planned each of our pregnancies. He had wanted children just as much as I had.

Ken was now in his own world of grief. As much as I wanted a re-assuring hug from him, he often could not give me one. I was placing myself, as the first and only person in this marriage who had lost a child.

Over time, I could admit that yes, men do grieve differently than women. With this admission, we made a huge step forward in our relationship. I had to let Ken grieve the loss of his daughter, not my daughter, in his own personal way. I had to be the one who saw when he needed a hug from me. I also had to be available to listen to him talk about his grief. It amazed me at how we each cherished different memories of Karen. We learned to combine them together as we reflected on her life.

How do we survive as a couple?

I found I had to give Ken what I wanted. If I wanted to be touched in a loving manner then I had to reach out physically to him. If I wanted him to smile at the dinner table and wipe the frown off his face, I had to smile at him.

We had spent so many years together as parents and then as empty nesters that when our world was turned upside down, we had to find anew what had attracted us to each other. What was it that attracted us to each other when we were teenagers? We had to find that connection again.

Over the years, we've allowed each other to grow and develop as our own unique persons. We've encouraged each other to pursue interests and hobbies. We've also tried and tested new interests that we can share together.

Three-and-a-half years after Karen died, Ken and I decided move to Park City. It was time for us to move on with our lives. We needed a new beginning, so we packed up everything and moved up the canyon. The move has given us a new and different outlook on life, and has had a very positive impact on our relationship. We love living in a resort community. A friend of mine once described Park City as "living in an adult day camp". I try to leave my problems at home when I go out. I know that Karen is watching us from somewhere on high and saying, "Way to go, Mom and Dad."

There have been times when I wondered if this marriage could survive the loss of our child. I admire Ken's commitment to me and this marriage. He is a very strong individual. Together we are stronger than when we stand alone. That is why God created marriage.

I believe we have survived by the grace of God. It is that plain and simple. Over time, I felt if God wanted us together, He would work things out between us.

Today Ken and I are still learning about one another as we approach our 40th anniversary. A little elasticity and flexibility in our relationship can go along way.

Chapter 4.

I sought out help within my community

In every community, there are resources to draw on when life gets difficult. All we have to do is look for them. I started by asking my friends for recommendations. Don't be afraid to seek out help. I am a much stronger person today because I sought help!

I seek help

There came a time in my life, before Karen became sick, when I began to remember being molested as a child in the early 1960's. I had suppressed the memories for over thirty-five years. Then in 1998, they came to the surface. I knew I needed professional help. I told Ken there was something from my childhood I needed to deal with; and he supported me.

I asked around, looking for a therapist. I asked a psychologist friend of ours if he could recommend anyone. I tried one counselor, but I knew it would not be a good fit. The name Donn Peters came up more than once.

One morning I called Dr. Peters' office. His voice on the answering machine sounded pleasant and caring, so I left a brief message. A few days later, we did a brief telephone interview, and I made an appointment to see him later that day. I liked him immediately; we just seemed to hit it off. So my counseling with Donn began in 1998.

I saw him weekly over the next few months. Donn showed all the patience in the world with me. He knew that when I was ready, I would open up about my molestation. One beautiful fall day I suggested we go for a walk outside. From that day on, relaxing walks became part of my therapy.

It was difficult for me to open up to Donn, as the sexual acts which took place when I was just thirteen seemed too private to discuss. Slowly over time, I did open up more and more with Donn as he put me at ease. I realized we had one common goal: dealing with my molestation memories and putting them to rest.

Little did either of us know we were laying the groundwork for years and years of therapy. Neither of us would have ever guessed what challenges would lay ahead of me.

Donn asked about my relationship with my daughter. I told him that Karen and I had had the typical mother-daughter struggles. We had tried counseling when she was in high school, but decided to work our problems out ourselves. Over the years, Karen and I had agreed on a mutual understanding.

As I progressed in counseling, Karen and I got along much better. The love never wavered between us, but our patience with each other did. Now my counseling was helping our relationship.

I called on Donn again from San Diego after my mother's fall. Over the next few months, Donn and I scheduled telephone counseling sessions. I continued to see him when I was in town. Donn was a huge support to me during this very trying time of my life.

Just when I thought my life was settling down again, it changed forever. Donn was on vacation on the east coast when I called his secretary and left a message about my daughter's cancer. I'll never forget when Donn returned my telephone call. Jane had taken Karen for a walk around the ward. For privacy, I curled up under Karen's hospital bed as I told him about Karen's cancer. Donn, as a parent, understood my feelings. All we could do was pray.

He would be there for my family as Karen fought her cancer. Finally, he came to my home to meet my family. Karen was full of optimism that day as were the rest of us.

Donn was a huge support as Karen fought her cancer. Ken, Brian and I saw him one day to discuss how we could be supportive of Karen in her cancer battle. I was now seeing him biweekly, as I was beside myself with churned up feelings. I would not admit to myself that I was scared to death. Death was not an option for Karen. We had a positive attitude full of hope. I kept Donn fully informed about Karen's health as she progressed with her cancer.

Then one day, I called Donn to cancel my appointment that afternoon. Karen's doctors wanted a conference with us at the hospital. Donn asked if I wanted him come. Of course, he did, and was with Ken, Brian and me when the doctors broke the news that Karen was dying. We were in total shock. I've never seen Donn's face so white. Ken and Brian's faces said it all too, total shock and disbelief.

Counseling plays an important role in my grief

As I faced life without Karen, Donn was there for me in my grief. Over the years, Donn and I have talked about so many subjects all of which had aided me in my struggles as I try to rebuild my new life.

As I grieved for Karen, I asked Donn if I was depressed. He told me I was distressed about Karen's death. That made a ton of sense to me. My grief journey has not been an easy one. I would not be the person I am today without Donn's guidance. He has been one of my main supporters as I write this book. In fact, he suggested it!

Donn and I have this little thing about "normal". Over the years, I asked him countless times; "Am I normal", in my grief or whatever issue we were discussing at the time. There have been times when he could almost see the question coming. One day I was at a craft store and bought a cute little sign that said, "Around here, "NORMAL" is just a setting on the washing machine". I bought it and took it to my next session with Donn. We both got a laugh out of it as I finally had the definition that I was looking for. Today the sign hangs in my laundry room.

"No, I will never be normal. My life is far from normal." There is no such thing as normal.

The grief support group

In my grief, I reached out to all the support groups I could find in my community. Many friends, doctors and pastors suggested a variety of groups. I found that at each group I attended, I learned something new. I was often the only one in the group who had lost an adult child.

The first year after Karen died. I went to "Compassionate Friends", a volunteer group of parents who have lost their children and support each other. I found this group very beneficial and full of suggestions about dealing with the loss of a child, but something was lacking. I still needed my weekly one on one therapy sessions with Donn.

When I was ready to read about grief, I scoured the public libraries, looking for books. I have always believed in home libraries so I began to buy books at an alarming rate. I have post-it notes and tabs in many books marking places that hit a nerve with me. Church libraries are another good source of self-help books.

There is no right or wrong way to grieve

The world is full of experts. They will tell you how and when to grieve, yet many of them do not have a clue what grief is all about. It takes all the patience I have at times not to lash out at the "know it alls" and ask, "Who have you lost?" I wonder if they should offer courses in tongue-biting in grief classes. I have learned over the years, it is the griever who has to change the most.

There is not a timetable when we grieve. Countless times, I have been asked "Are you over it yet?" This happened when it had only been six weeks since Karen died! I had to remind myself the person did not understand the impact of loss.

I used to say there was no such word as "never." Then, Karen died and I met it. In grief, we meet the word "never". We will "never" hear their voice again. We will "never" see them again. We will "never" have our dreams for our loved one fulfilled. We have hit a brick wall at 300 miles an hour. The force of this crash can be unbearable, yet we will find a way to move on. It has taken me a long time to realize I will "never" see her again.

As I have walked down the path of my grief, I have learned and met many new challenges so let us look at them now.

Chapter 5.

Learning to meet new challenges

🎵🎵

With every new experience, growth will come. Grief is no exception.

I have a lot to learn

We all need food in the house if we are to eat. I can only tolerate so much takeout. Going to the grocery store for the first time after Karen died was a new experience. As I walked into the store, it seemed to be filled with mothers and daughters. I could hear them talking about the meals they were planning. Then I looked down and saw Karen's favorite cereal. I lost it. The tears ran down my face. I stood alone in the store aisle, overcome with grief. The sight of Honey Nut Cheerios brought back so many memories of Karen. I prayed no one would walk down the aisle. I knew I had to pull myself together if only for brief moment while I shopped. I didn't want to explain my distress to anyone. I wanted to abandon my grocery cart and run for the privacy of my car, but I knew I could not.

I faced another challenge as I checked out with my full cart. Why do store checkers always say "How are you?" and "Have a nice day?" With my mascara running down my face and swollen eyes, I was in no mood for either. I just wanted to punch her out and say "No I am not having a nice day. My daughter died recently so why should I be Miss Happy Customer?" Instead, I ignored her remarks and left the store as calmly as possible. When I got to the car, I let the tears come.

Everyday in grief, I faced new challenges. Just venturing outside my door was a new experience. Aside from the gas station, everywhere I went I found myself interacting with people. I learned to slough off "Have a nice day" or "How are you?" Did they really care? I believe it's just a social expression we all use.

I was tempted on my playful days to ask, "Do you really want to know? I'll be happy to tell you: my dog died a year ago, my aging mother now lives near me and I have to look after her and to top it off my daughter died last month." This would make some store clerks rethink asking the question.

One of the most painful lessons I have had to learn is how to control my harsh tongue. I wanted so many times to lash out because I was in so much pain. I was learning a new vocabulary along with my grief. Now I needed to put the knowledge I was learning in my grief support classes and from Donn into action. Yes, I could smile at the grocery store checker and agree with her as I practiced my social skills.

Going out to lunch with my friends can be trying when all they want to do is talk about their grandchildren. I love the fellowship of getting together, but I wanted to scream, "Give me a break! Karen has just died and I won't have any grandchildren from her." Oh, everyone once in while I said some sly comment to change the subject, but most often my comments went unnoticed. I learned to just sit there and smile.

I learned very fast that I was the one who had to change and for my own good, I needed to do it fast. Remember how the rain runs off your umbrella on a rainy day? I would imagine that my back was an umbrella and I'd let hurtful comments just run off my back and onto the floor.

Other days I imagined I was a turtle. Turtles have hard shells protecting their soft bodies. They can crawl into their shell for safety and stick their heads out when they want to explore the world. Many days I was brave and stuck my head outside into the world at large. Then when my feelings got hurt, I would crawl back inside my shell. Some days I'd stay in there for a very long time. I learned over time when I stayed in there for more than three days, I would get myself into trouble. As I learned more about myself on my grief journey, I learned that when I was down in the dumps more than three days, I was stuck in the muck of my grief: a place I didn't want to be. This is when I knew I had to find away back into life. So, as time went by, I began to stick my head out more and more. I will always have the safety of my shell, but who wants to live there all the time?

The holidays and making new traditions

One of the first things I learned about grief was that I'd have to face holidays and my child's birthday and her death anniversary with a totally new and different outlook on life.

Mother's Day: This was the first holiday I had to face after Karen died. I faced it within weeks of her death. Jane stepped in and kept Ken and me so busy that we hardly had time to remember it was Mother's Day. Thank goodness for life-saving friends.

I sailed through the first summer without much trouble. Then, as the stores started putting out the Christmas merchandise, I grew restless. How would I face Thanksgiving and Christmas? At least I could look forward to Brian coming home for Christmas. This was a gift in itself.

Ken and I discussed how we would remember Karen at Christmas. Then I recalled that Karen had given Ken and me the most unusual gift for the past two Christmases. She knew we could buy what we wanted so she decided to do a Sub for Santa as her gift to us. Ken and I had felt so honored to receive this gift. Karen had really grown up with the values we had hoped she would.

Most communities have charity organizations that will have needy families that you can "adopt" and give them a Christmas they wouldn't have without assistance. In our community this is called "Sub for Santa." This is done anonymously.

So I suggested, "This is a wonderful idea! Why don't we continue it?" Brian agreed that it would be a new and wonderful tradition to start as we remember Karen by giving to the less fortunate at Christmas. Now when Christmas rolls around, I contact a charity and ask for a needy family with whom we can share Christmas. It is a family affair as we shop and wrap the gifts for that family. I know Karen is watching from above and smiling down at us as we shed a tear or two in her memory.

When the New Year rolled around, I was so happy. I had lived through more than I thought one life could stand in the past year. I looked to the New Year with anticipation and a smile.

January brought Karen's birthday. How would I get through it? Then five days later, it was our anniversary. Karen's birthday overshadowed our anniversary the first year, so I made a vow to try to keep each separate. Without my anniversary, I would not have had Karen. Just the same, I was very restless on Karen's birthday. I decided to make it a "Jan day" and relax with a massage along with some pampering.

I dreaded the approach of spring when nature would open up with new life, as it would mark one year without Karen. I was on new and foreign soil, and wondered how I would make it through this day. One day, that was never supposed to happen in my life. I reminded myself time and time again that I had to take one day at a time.

Karen's anniversary did come. Ken and I went our separate ways as we remembered Karen. We needed time to be alone. Then we went out for dinner together.

Looking back at all the firsts, I have learned that the anticipation of them is harder than the actual day. My nerves were on high alert as the day was approaching, and so I was extra sensitive. When the day finally arrived, I was relieved it had come and was now almost past. I learned that planning ahead can made these tough days flow easier.

I know myself well enough to know I am extra sensitive around the holidays. Holidays can be what we want them to be. I protect myself by giving myself three days before the actual holiday to relax and comfort myself. I will not take on any extra projects. I become the project myself. I also need to make sure I give Ken the space he needs.

The shock is now beginning to wear off

We enjoy the ride so much better in a car with shock absorbers. I believe God created emotional shock as a way of cushioning our lives. Now with the shock of the death of our child, God thought we slowly needed to ease into the acceptance of the reality that our child was gone. So He created shock.

In the months following Karen's death, I was in a fog bank, but you could not tell me that at the time. I thought I was doing great. Then after the first Christmas without Karen and as her birthday approached in January, I realized the shock of her death was slowly wearing off. I was coming back to reality. My daughter was dead. It was not until this time that I could really say Karen was dead and understand it in my mind. Now, I knew she was gone, but dead? I still had a hard time comprehending it.

Over the next few months as I looked back at how I had handled my grief in the past. I saw that keeping my head in the fog bank was a way of protecting me from myself.

I realized shock does protect our mind as we learn to adjust to the changes in our lives. Now I could move forward on my grief journey in a much healthier manner. I began to see some of the mistakes I had made.

Learning from the mistakes

Wow, life is full of adventure. However, grief was one adventure I could have done without. Since I got the ticket into grief, I had to stop and look at where I had been and what I could learn from my mistakes.

Yes, I had cruelly spouted off more than once at a person. Now I had to decide if I needed to apologize to anyone I had offended. Was that person important enough in my life? I apologized to several friends, and probably forgot to apologize to one or two friends, but I saw no point in going back to the sales clerk who had probably forgotten who I was.

I believe when we admit we made a mistake we are taking a huge step forward in life. Not everyone can admit to making a mistake. Our apology has to come from the heart or it will be useless and the receiver will see through it.

In our society, grief is not understood, and so many people misinterpret what the griever is trying to say. After all how much experience have we had in grief? My grief did not come with an instruction book.

As the time wore on, I realized I had to change some of my actions, including what I said. I had to take ownership of my grief. When necessary, I had to pick up the telephone or visit the person I had offended and make my apologies to them.

Yes, we can and should rise above our pain as we journey down our road to acceptance that we have lost our child. It is never easy to admit our mistakes, but it is part of life.

I can't fill the void with material belongings

There is a hole in my heart, a hole in my life. It will never be replaced. All the same, I have tried.

I love to shop. There was a time after Karen died that I became a mall rat. I visited some stores on a weekly basis. Many of the sales clerks even knew me by name. I tried to shop away my grief. I bought things that were not me and that I knew I would not wear, but there was the thrill of the hunt and the bargain-basement price tag.

At the end of the month, I saw the credit card bills. In a grief class, one instructor said, "Freeze your credit cards. Then think about the purchase you want make as you defrost the card." Do I really want or need this purchase? It took me a long time to realize that I cannot fill the void left by Karen by shopping.

We need to protect our wallets and more importantly our minds. We need to find useful and creative ways to fill the void.

I have a healthier out look on life now

I love to look nice; it is part of who I am. Many times I have walked into Donn's office and fooled him by how I look. The old saying "Don't judge a book by its cover" applies to me as well. I have thrown Donn for a loop more than once.

We all have window dressings. When I look good, I feel good. Some days I can even fool myself. When I fool myself on the outside, I begin to fool myself on the inside and this soon can become a healthy habit.

I love having clean windows in my house. This brightens my spirit, but more importantly my soul. When my soul is in balance, I project a positive me. A positive self can rub off on Ken.

I like doing little surprise things for others. Yet, I have a hard time accepting a complement. Why is this? I was aware of a negative outlook on life in my childhood home. So as an adult I have had to work hard to overcome this personal flaw. I would much rather be around people with a positive outlook and this begins with me.

Mirrors can tell us so much. They can tell us how we look on the outside when we least expect it. Now the internal mirror, the one that reflects our heart, is the one that really counts; if our spirit is shinning bright on the inside of our souls, it shines through our body out into the world. This is the person I want to be and be around, don't you?

Chapter 6.

I have to draw in my inner strength

A s human beings, we all have feelings. Now, I was learning to listen more and more to my soul. I alone have to decide what is best for me; no one can do it for me. The world is full of armchair quarterbacks who want to give us advice on something they have heard or read. In the end, this is my grief, my loss. I have to decide how I want to live my life.

I count my blessings

Did you watch the sunset last night? Did you watch the sunrise this morning? Did you take a hot bath or shower within the last 48 hours? Did you flush the toilet today? Then you must have running water in the house. If you had time or the luxury of doing any of these, then you are one of the privileged in the world.

I have to stop regularly and count my blessings. I have the sight to see so many wonderful things in this world. One of the first signs that there was something wrong with Karen was that she lost the sight in her left eye. But she never considered herself even partially blind. This was not a handicap to her. It was a way of life that she had to accommodate to.

So I count my blessings. Karen enriched my life for 31 years. She showed me things I would have never known.

The next time you see a daisy, take it in your hand and count your blessings, one petal at a time. The blessings can be about today, your family or memories of your child. I always find this small act soothes my soul and calms my nerves.

I love the wonders of nature. I often pause a moment just to look out the window and see what is new in my world. This small act refreshes my day. I often find a new wildflower outside my window or see new animal tracks. Our world is constantly changing.

Gratitude can go a long way in life

Donn has encouraged me many times to write a gratitude journal. There is something magical about putting our words on paper.

Today I am grateful that I have a computer on which to write my book. I am also grateful I have electricity in my home, a roof over my head, and beautiful scenery out my window.

When we start to think about all the things for which we can be grateful, we are showing our appreciation for our life. When we express our gratitude about our lives, the list suddenly starts to go on and on without end.

There were many days, early on my grief journey, when gratitude was the farthest thing from my mind. What did I have to be grateful for? I wanted the missing link back in my life. At those times, I had to remind myself to be grateful for having Karen grace my life as long as she did.

A little gratitude can go a long way. Gratitude can spread like a wildfire in our lives, a fire that we can let burn forever. So light the match of gratitude in your life. Let the flame burn bright, each and every day.

Crying with a box of tissues

When it comes to grieving, crying is a no-brainer.

When was the last time you had a good cry, an all-out meltdown? The experts tell us crying is healing. Crying can cleanse the soul and heart. If crying did cause eye damage, I would have gone blind!

At first, I was self-conscious about crying. Donn taught me a valuable lesson in a therapy session when he said, "Jan you don't have to explain to anyone why you are crying". That made sense to me. He was right; I didn't have to explain to anyone. Crying is a normal part of grief!

I also found staring out the window to be soothing. What matters is that we are comfortable and have the privacy we need to process our tears. I've sat by my window for hours without moving a muscle and stared out at nothing, and found this ritual to be healing.

As a grieving mother, I should have bought stock in a tissue company. I see nothing wrong with giving a griever a case of tissue as a sympathy gift instead of flowers. One of the first purchases we had to make at a warehouse store was a case of tissue. I have those small packets of tissue in almost every purse I own. Need a tissue? Ask me!

I am still an open crier. I can cry anywhere at any time. I am no longer embarrassed about it. On days I am more susceptible to my grief, I do not wear mascara. I'm still looking for the perfect mascara, but nothing can survive the rain storm of grief when I cry.

Limiting my pity parties

There is a difference between grief and pity. In grief we have suffered a loss we may be distressed and have sorrow. With pity, there maybe sympathetic sorry evoked by the suffering of another. When we are in pain it maybe hard for us to recognize the difference between these two works. I found myself falling into the pity mode so often.

Have you ever been invited to a party you did not want to attend? Self-pity is one such party. When Karen died, I often found myself in a fast-moving spiral into a pity party.

I wanted to invite everyone with me. I invited Ken, Brian, Donn, Jane and whoever else whom I thought might want to come with me. Eventually I learned the party was meant for only me. I had been to this party many times as I worked through my molestation. It was always the same: I sank deeper and deeper into the muck of despair, feeling sorry for myself. As I focused on why I was in this terrible state of mind, I became enraged at life. I wallowed in self-pity.

My self-pity began usually when I let myself become worn down. Over time I've learned to recognize the warning signs of an invitation to this party. So I stop and ask myself if I want to go to a pity party? I remind myself that I can drown there. When I think about it, I can often stop myself before I get in the swing of the party. This is called growth in grief.

Donn and I have discussed pity parties many times in our therapy sessions. Slowly over time, I began to realize how unhealthy they were. Yes, I could go for a short time but it was dangerous for me to take up residence and stay for any length of time.

It is so easy to fall into the pity party trap when we lose our child. The triggers that set up my party can be something insignificant, and yet my mind lets me get so worked up until everything is blown out of proportion.

Just the other day, I let myself get so worked up over something, I found myself at a pity party. I made myself stop and ask, "Is this where I want to be? Is this the right way to handle the problem in my head? Is this worth the stress on my body? Do I really want to visit this place? How long do I want to stay? Can I afford to stay?" When I recognized the triggers and the side effects, then I could begin to heal myself. Another way, I show progress is when I pull myself out of the muck of my grief. I am making great strides forward in my life.

Putting away the gold star of grief

Remember, on the old TV show "Gun Smoke," when Matt Dillon wore his gold marshal's star? In the early days of my grief journey, I wore a gold star myself. My gold star was about the death of my daughter. I wanted to tell everyone I met about the tragic loss of my daughter. The loss became my identity. I was in such pain I wanted to share it with the world!

When someone said they were having a bad day, I would tell them my day was worse than theirs and why. My gold star became my way of asking for sympathy. Over time, I saw how others wore the traumas of their lives on their chest, too. One day I thought, "Do I want to be known as a grieving mother? No. Do I want to wear my grief on my chest for all to see? No. Do I want to keep my pain in my heart, as I learn to live with it? No. Do I want be thought of as a bitter grieving mother in ten years? No."

Slowly, over time, I realized I needed to shed my "poor-me" attitude. I wanted to be thought of as a strong woman. I would let others wonder why I was sympathetic, and kind, perhaps.

So I decided to put my gold star in my dresser drawer. This imaginary act was my way of saying I no longer wanted to share my grief with the world. I found when I humbled myself to others they reacted in a positive way to me. I realized this was a huge step forward in my learning to accept my life the way it is today. I was beginning to see the light. I needed to live my life for me.

My blessing was that I had had the privilege of knowing my daughter.

Karen is no longer in pain, so why am I?

At first after Karen's death, I thought I had to do everything in my life in memory of Karen. Then slowly I realized I had to do it for me, not Ken or Brian but me. I made more strides in my healing journey when I asked myself why I was in pain when Karen was no longer in pain. I still had a lot of living left in my life. This was a real wake-up call for me.

When I ask myself, "Karen is no longer in pain why am I suffering so?" I answer, "I love her, and I always will." Because we love, we will suffer. Karen would not want me to suffer and focus on her death. Karen would want me to live life to the fullest. I should not do it in her memory but for me. This is when I began to move forward with my life.

Incorporating grief in my life

Years ago, I was a smoker, but I quit in the early 1990's. In the late 1990's, I was diagnosed with mild emphysema and asthma. All my years of smoking had caught up with me. A friend who suffered from an enlarged heart gave me great advice: "Learn to incorporate your asthma and emphysema into your life so others will not know you have these conditions." That made sense. I could make lifestyle adjustments as I protected my health and others would not be aware of what I was doing.

I followed her advice. I learned the symptoms that trigger my stressful breathing, when I needed to protect myself, and when I could use my inhaler for relief. I learned that I had to avoid smokers and heavy perfume.

I began to apply the same principal to my grief. It became my goal to incorporate Karen's death into my life so people would not know that I was a grieving mother. How did I do this? Here are some examples: I don't want guests in my home to feel as if they are drowning in my grief, or even to know that I've lost a child. So I do not have family pictures in the public rooms of my house. I have the largest display—nine pictures, three of which are of Karen only—on a bookcase in my office. I also have her small tabletop harp on the bookcase. These are my personal reminders of my family's history. In the bedrooms, there are small pictures of my children.

I do have small personal reminders of my love for each of my children. Throughout my house, you will find a yellow rose. We had one yellow rose at Karen's memorial for each year she lived, and let her friends take one at the end of the service. Today yellow roses have special meaning for my family. When someone asks me who made the cross stitch of Bless This House, I simply say, "My daughter."

Years ago, I decided to place the centerpiece of dining table where Karen used to sit. Now, it is just a matter of habit for me to leave the centerpiece there. This is an example of the little things we can do around the house to make the void less noticeable.

Over the years, I've learned to make general references about my children. I talk about my daughter in the past tense and about my son in the present tense. Very few people ever catch this.

I used to stumble when people asked me, "How many children do you have?" I didn't want to go into details about Karen's death nor did I want to ignore her presence in my life. Quite often, I would just say two, and then change the subject, asking about their family.

When I am out with friends, I've learned to keep my memories to myself. This way I don't drown them with talking about my deceased daughter, nor do I have to share about her life. It still amazes me how we always talk about the living and not the dead. Anyway, I often let the conversation just go with the flow. Some would say I have become quieter than

I used to be. My reply to that is I just have become more selective in the subject I wish to discuss.

We all have baggage in life regardless of our age. I want to be respected for who I am today, not where I have been or who I was six years ago. I am not the same person I was then.

I have learned from my past, as I plan and look forward to the future. I will never forget my past. It has allowed me to build the strength I need today as I move forward and bloom with each new experience. Just watch me grow now.

As I look at my past life experience I can learn from them as I grow into the future.

Chapter 7.

Learning about grief from my past

There are many types of grief, not all are due to a death. We can have the grief of ending a friendship, or a marriage that ends. I have even grieved when we sold our boat, knowing I would miss the good times. I grieved when we moved out of San Diego in the early 1970's. Grief can take many forms. It's helpful to think about how grief has played a role in your life.

As a child, I learned about grief through my pets and the loss of a grandparent.

Learning about grief when my pets died

When I was six years old, I got a goldfish. My parents thought this would teach me responsibility. It was my job to clean out the fish bowl. As the weeks went by, I watched my goldfish. My fish was a pet that I could observe but not touch. When I got lazy and forgot to clean the bowl, my parents scolded me. One day, my fish was floating upside down. My parents had told me if this happened, it meant the fish had died. I decided to bury my gold fish via the garbage disposal.

Within a few days I had another fish. I kept the bowl clean this time, but as I was cleaning the bowl, the gold fish slipped away down the kitchen drain. I was devastated! How could this happen? Over the next year, I said hello and good-bye to several fish.

One day, I decided I wanted a turtle. My mom took me to the local pet store, and I bought my turtle with my allowance along with a clear plastic bowl and a green palm tree. I thought I was the luckiest kid on the block. I could hold my turtle in my hand for a brief time as long as I kept it wet. One day my turtle died.

I wanted a real pet, but was unsuccessful at convincing my parents. One day, a fat cat plopped herself down on our front porch seeking shelter from the rain. The cat hung around for several days, thanks to my secretly giving her milk.

This is how Winnie came to live with us. Several weeks later, Winnie gave birth to kittens in my father's closet. Over the next few years, I learned about birth and death. If we lost a kitten, I buried it under a tree in the backyard. When my parents built a new garage many years later, I thought of all the pets I had buried there as a child. I have never forgotten them.

One day my mother decided she wanted a dog. We got a beagle. Unfortunately the cat and dog did not get along. A month later, my mother said, "They both have to go. I cannot live like this." I'll never forget my dad loading up the car with them. I was nine years old, and I was heart broken!

I didn't know it at the time, but I was grief stricken at losing my pets. I moped around the house for days and weeks. I was told someday we would get another pet. This was of little consequence to me at the time.

Over the years, I have had five dogs. Today Pepper, our chocolate Labrador, often lends his moral support as I write. To me, a house is not a home without a dog.

Biscuit, our yellow Labrador, was my dog. We adopted him when he was three months old from the humane society, two weeks after we lost Brandy, the black Labrador of our children's childhood. Biscuit was the first of our empty-nest dogs. He and I were pet partners who volunteered and did animal therapy for many years.

Biscuit graced our lives for ten years before he developed cancer in June 2000. We had to put Biscuit to sleep ten months before Karen died. Pepper came to live at our house two weeks later, just in time for the 4th of July 2000. I was still grieving for Biscuit when we got Pepper.

As an adult, I usually grieved for my dogs for two years after their deaths. Each of their deaths was unbearable for me. I was a zombie after they died. Yet we went out and got their replacement right away. As each dog came and went, I said, "I can never love another dog as much." Yet, somehow, I manage to fall in love all over again with a new personality.

I think the death of my dogs prepared me more than any other death for the most horrendous death yet to come.

Grandparents will die

I was fortunate to spend many happy, carefree days as a child with each of my grandparents, and I have many happy memories.

I was in high school when one of my grandfathers died of a heart condition. In my 20's, one of my grandmothers and my other grandfather died. My other grandmother died when I was in my 30's. With each of these deaths, I shed a few tears, but accepted this as a part of the life cycle. They had each lived a full life. Since each of them passed away without suffering a major disease, my family felt blessed.

The old will die and the young will mature and grow old. The order of death in nature is this will happen. None of us escapes this world alive.

Sooner or later our parents will die

The day will come when we have to say good-bye to our parents; hopefully, this will occur after they have lived a long and fulfilling life. By now most of us will have reached middle age ourselves.

My dad was fortunate. He died in his sleep of a heart condition. Dad had a heart condition for many years, so when mom called to say he had died in the middle of the night; I was saddened but not surprised. We were all grateful he did not suffer through a long drawn out illness. Quick was the way he would have wanted it.

My mother would outlive my dad by twenty years. Both of my parents had quality lives.

When I look back at their lives, I have to celebrate and remember them as people who contributed to this world each in their own unique way. I'm grateful my children had the opportunity to know their grandparents. This added to the quality of each of their lives.

With each person and death my life has been enriched I have learned something with each experience. Each of them has left an imprint upon my life.

Then the unthinkable death happened.

Our children aren't suppose to die

We have words — widow and widower — to indicate a person whose spouse has died. Divorce indicated a marriage has ended. Orphan is a word to describe a child who has lost his or her parents. Yet we have no word to describe the parent whose child has died. "Childless" does not work, because we have had a child and in many ways we still do. After I lost Karen, I decided there was no word to describe the loss because the loss is far too great to be encompassed by one word.

A child's death is out of the natural sequence of life. Grandparents die. Parents die. Even we will die, when we reach old age. But children? No. We are not supposed to bury our young!

To lose a child is out of the sequence of life. Older members of society die first. When we are children, our grandparents may die. When we are adults, our parents, who are now around the age our grandparents were, will die. One day, when we've aged like our grandparents and parents before us, we, too, will die. But life has thrown some of us a curve ball and our children have died before us. This is not part of the normal progression of life. We are not supposed to bury our young!

Learning from Karen's experiences of death

So now the question in my mind became, what can I learn from Karen's life and death? How can I use what I have learned from my daughter as I struggle to go on with my life?

I decided early on in my grief to calm my broken heart by remembering that Karen lived a very complete and full life in her 31 years. She graduated college in three years, but still was not satisfied, so studied another year and a half to earn a second degree. She was one of the greatest teachers I know. She was a teacher by profession, but more importantly, she was a natural teacher to those around her. She was always sharing her vast knowledge with everyone who met her. Karen was always full of life, eagerly looking forward to the next adventure.

As I watched her fight against cancer, not knowing she would die in such a short time, I learned about courage facing the unknown. In those short seven weeks, I saw inner strength and determination. When Karen was a teenager, I told her, "Karen, you are a stick of dynamite in a small package". When she was diagnosed with cancer, she used that strength to battle her cancer.

Karen had a dream of beating her cancer and becoming a coach for others fighting cancer. She never got the chance to share her knowledge, but she did show courage! I think this is one of the reasons I have chosen to write this book. It is my way of continuing Karen's legacy.

When she died, I had to learn how to face my unknown future without her presence in my life. The strength she showed has become an example of how I must not give up on life.

Karen would want me to go on and live a full life. I focused on this and then slowly came to realize that I had to honor her by living my life for me.

I had to remind myself that I still had something to give this world. There were times I wasn't sure what, and Donn would remind me that I was still a woman of great strength. I had survived a mother who chose not to be present for me. I had survived the unwelcome hands of my molester. Many of the trials of my life I had kept inside for many years as I suffered in silence.

Now, with Karen's death, it was time for me to share my pains with others so I could heal my wounded heart. My goal, ultimately, was to learn how to incorporate knowing my daughter into my life. This is not an easy goal to accomplish; it takes constant awareness and sometimes a real struggle. I often have to remind myself, "Yes, I am worth it." There is still a lot of living for me to do. I still have a lot left in me to give this world

But I can't do it alone. I need God in my life. After all, he is the silent partner in my life.

Chapter 8.

Where is God in my life?

Ken and I have gone to church all of our married life. We raised our children in the Christian church. The anonymous tale called "Footprints," below, describes my walk with Jesus during my grief journey.

"Footprints"

One night a man had a dream. He dreamed he was walking along the beach with the LORD. Across the sky flashed scenes from his life. For each scene, he noticed two sets of footprints in the sand; one belonging to him, and the other to the LORD. When the last scene of his life flashed before him, he looked back at the footprints in the sand. He noticed that many times along the path of his life there was only one set of footprints. He also noticed that it happened at the very lowest and saddest times of his life. This really bothered him and he questioned the LORD about it. "LORD, you said that once I decided to follow you, you'd walk with me all the way. But I have noticed that during the most troublesome times in my life, there is only one set of footprints. I don't understand why when I need you most you would leave me." The LORD replied. "My precious, precious child, I love you and I would never leave you. During your times of trial and suffering when you see only one set of footprints, it was then that I carried you."

Author unknown

God carries me

"During your times of trial and suffering when you see only one set of footprints, it was I then that I carried you." This is and has been one of the most profound statements to describe how I feel about my walk with Jesus since Karen's death. I've had so many people ask me how I do it. I have two responses: "By the grace of God" or I tell them about "Footprints" and the last sentence of the poem.

Yes, the Lord does carry me when I least expect it, when I do not have the strength to go it on my own.

He is comforting me

The first year or so I think I went through the motions of being a Christian. I went to church every week. I tried to attend Bible Studies. I think I went for the fellowship with others. I went through the motions of being a Christian. It took me a long time to realize the Lord was there for me as he always had been. I was in too much pain to see and feel his presence with me.

I will never forget a therapy session with Donn when I stopped our conversation and said, "Do you feel it? He is here with us! I can feel Him around the two of us." Donn and I were sitting in a corner chair arrangement in his office, talking about God's role in my life when He made His presence known to me. I believe Donn also felt His presence that day.

I have felt the comforting arms of Jesus around me many times when I least expected it, like a loving parent holding me as I grieved my daughter.

I have to remind myself that Mary wept at the foot of the cross when Jesus was on it. Yes, God knows my pain. He too saw His child die.

He understands my anger

I believe God created us. He gave us anger, and He is able to take it when we lash back at Him. If God can give us this emotion, then He can take it when we feel it, since He feels our pain, too. He also understood my disappointment as I watched Karen die of cancer. He also lost a daughter when Karen died.

So when I shouted and raged with my anger about *why* Karen got cancer, I must remind myself that from the beginning of time in the Garden of Eden, we have lived in a fallen world. The answer to *"why"* is, I do not have to try to rationalize it or try to justify it. I just have to learn to accept it.

We are all equal at the foot of the cross. This really levels the playing field. Jesus weeps with us!

I have to ask for His help

Jesus never closed the door on me. I tried to close the door on Him, as I just went though the motions of living my faith. Jesus has all the patience in the world. He stands quietly in the wings off stage waiting for me to invite Him back on to the main stage of my life. He knew that when I was ready, I would come back to His loving arms.

Ken and I had attended the same church for twenty years. About two and half years after Karen died, when my feelings were hurt badly, we left that church. The why is not important, the results are. We visited and then joined another Lutheran church in Salt Lake City. It was at our new church that I really began to feel Jesus at work in my life. One Wednesday night after attending Lenten Service, I went straight home and wrote the following.

"Meeting Jesus"

"Have you ever thought what it will be like when we meet Jesus? I thought and wondered about this one evening as I sat at an Ash Wednesday Lenten Service. I know Karen, my daughter, had her faith in Jesus Christ. Karen knew exactly where she was going as her life support was being removed. Karen was going into the arms of Jesus. She did wave "goodbye" to us and I like to think "hello" to Jesus when she passed into His arms. I can just imagine His loving arms reaching out to greet Karen and every new person entering heaven. Just the thought of His loving arms reaching out to her and all of us is such a wonderful comforting thought. Close your eyes. Can you imagine and feel His wonderful arms around you now?

Now let's think a little further. Let's think about ourselves being welcomed into heaven. I want to be welcomed and hugged by Jesus. I'm lost. I'm new at this. I want someone to show me the way. I am also very confused as to the protocol. Now what? It is my hope that Jesus would invite me to partake of communion with Him. Jesus would give the sacraments to me. He would serve me and forgive all of my sins. I would be surrounded by my family members and loved ones who have gone before me. It would be a time of great celebration with Jesus at the head of the table. I would be in total amazement at the whole celebration! After all, we do sing, "This is the Feast and Celebration*" when we prepare to receive *communion. This would be the real thing. It would be the welcoming into my eternal home with Jesus.*

I would once again be in the presence of Karen just as it had been told to me for so long. Now it would be true. Karen would be there as my guide into my new eternal life.

It would be such joy and adventure to discover heaven with my daughter as my guide. The thought of this gives me hope and comfort.

Close your eyes now and let your mind drift again. Can you feel Jesus now? He is sitting right here with me as I type this. I can feel him comforting me now. He is holding me ever so gently. Oh, how I treasure these moments....... "

> In memory of Karen Jaworski, who lost her life to cancer at the age of 31 in 2001
> By Jan Jaworski 2/25/04.
> In the Lutheran Book of Worship

I wrote "Meeting Jesus," long before I ever dreamed of writing a book. Today whenever I read it, I want to cry again. It is my hope that sharing it with you helps you find comfort also, by placing your child's name in place of Karen's.

Yes, when I ask Jesus for His help, He is, and always will be, there for me.

God laughs and cries with me

Jesus has to have a sense of humor, after all He created me. I am sure there have been many times in my life when He has laughed at me, particularly in my grief journey.

There was the time I was driving between Jane's house and the pharmacy rushing to get home to Karen. A policeman pulled me over for speeding in a residential area. The officer asked if I knew how fast I was going. I said, "No." Then I told him my life story, ending with where I had been and where I was going. The officer must have thought no one could makeup a story like that, so he let me go with only a verbal warning. Thank God. I'm sure He was protecting me and proving to me that honesty does pay.

My sense of humor was on hold after Karen died. I have never had a great sense of humor in the first place, so I was lucky when it started to come back. Today I am quick with one liner's. I enjoy catching people off guard.

Jesus and I have a good cry now and then. He must have just had a good laugh just now when I typed dry for cry. Yes, he does dry my tears away quite often.

Jesus can be my best friend when I invite Him into my life. Sometimes I only want Him to be with me. I enjoy being alone and what better company to invite than Jesus? He understands my thoughts and my logic, which can be a challenge for everyone else. I find comfort when I spend time alone with Him. Some days we just sit by the window or we go for a walk. Spending time with Him, who understands all my many moods, whether laughing or crying, lifts my spirits and nourishes my soul. It is when I do not spend time with Him that my life gets out of balance and I go wacky.

Life is a journey. I do it better when I walk hand in hand with Jesus.

Chapter 9.
I don't want to forget Karen

✿ ✿

The memories of Karen are impossible for me to forget. She is part of me and always will be, wherever she lives. But I never dreamed she would live only in my heart.

Pictures create a mental puzzle for me. A couple of years after Karen died, I put together a small photo album to show friends whom I had not seen in years. It was a history of my family, not just a photo album of Karen. I went through all the family pictures I'd stored in photo boxes over the years. This album was a labor of love.

We were always great ones to take snapshots. In my grief, I found it very difficult to look at them. We have so many of the pictures are of Karen and Brian together. I have a few of just Karen alone. Our family was so closely intertwined it is hard to separate us. I find comfort in knowing where pictures are in my house. Some day, perhaps, I will put them together in a larger photo album, but for the time being, I can wait.

I sustain myself with the pictures of Karen in my mind, along with a few I have in my office.

I have to remind myself reliving isn't healthy

I hope and pray Karen does not remember the last few days of her life now that she's in heaven. Her mind was alert until that last moment of her life. I hope she left the earth with only pleasant memories of her time here.

Yet, the last days of her life are ingrained in my mind, as are the last seven weeks of her life. I can't tell you how many times I have replayed those days. The first couple of years after Karen left; I rewound my memories when the anniversary of her illness and death came around on the calendar. I have an instant recall of watching her suffer, and yet I cherished the time with her as I told her repeatedly how much I loved her.

If love is the motivator that carries me through my grief, there is one piece of this puzzle missing. Is it healthy for me to relive the pain of watching her suffer? NO. Would Karen want me to stay focused on her suffering? NO.

Donn watched me suffer so many times in our therapy sessions that he finally asked, "Jan, is it healthy for you to hang onto those memories of Karen's last few days?" He knew the images I had in my mind. He had visited Ken and me at the hospital four of Karen's last five days with us. So when he asked that, out of concern for me, I knew the answer was NO.

I still had one major memory that caused me to feel the pain of her suffering. Could I find a way in my heart to let those memories of Karen go? I had to for my own well-being. Letting go of seeing Karen on life support and waving good-bye was one of the most painful aspects of my grief.

The two areas of Karen's body where the cancer had not invaded were her brain and the heart. These are the two areas of my body that suffer the most with the acceptance: in my brain as my aching heart yearns for her.

Today, something will trigger my mind back to those final days and I know that I can visit them briefly but I can't let my mind stay. Karen would not want me to get lost in the mechanics of her death. Nor would she want me to mourn for her.

I need to celebrate Karen's life now

As I reflect back on Karen's life, I need to remember the good times. I need to be thankful for the many wonderful experiences we shared together, even our struggles, because we each grew with them.

I am proud of the child she was and woman she became. I beam with joy when I meet someone who knew Karen and they tell me what a wonderful person she was. I love to hear Karen stories; I learn more about who she was. Karen's personality made people remember her. She had a way of making people feel so special. We were once on the beach at a street fair in San Diego when Ken ran into someone who had met Karen at a social event. He remembered Karen's playing the harp and how it touched him so. I remind myself that Karen's memory lives on in the lives of the people she touched.

I learned so much about the world through Karen's eyes and spirit. Today, I need to celebrate the spirit of her life that remains within me. One way I can do this is by incorporating her strength into my life. As the wind blew through her long hair, so her spirit blows through me now.

Can I afford the weight of my grief on my shoulders?

Can I afford a twenty-ton weight on my shoulders? There are many days I do carry one, but can I afford to? No. Do I want my mental attitude to reflect my pain? There have been times that I feel as if I were oozing grief through my pores. Is this how I want to project my self-image? No.

I often wonder why I continue to carry that weight. I have thought that perhaps I was a slow learner in grief, but I know now that is not the answer. I realize that, somewhere inside, I think I will dishonor Karen if I don't hang onto the weight of her broken life.

Ken often asks me how you eat an elephant. I reply, "One bite at a time." This is the wisdom I've learned to lighten the weight of Karen's death from my life. I can't just do it in one large spill like a dump truck. I have to do it slowly, over time.

Why was I holding on to the weight? My shoulders and back were aching. I wanted to feel light as a feather and be a free spirit like I had been years ago.

I will find ways to honor Karen's life

Every day I remind myself that I must honor Karen's life. It can be the simplest thing, such as smiling at the clouds passing by or blowing Karen a butterfly kiss. I have to remind myself when I am out and about, when I see mothers and daughters having a good time, that I should celebrate it with them in my mind. I want to tell to them, "Cherish every moment, because you don't know when you will have the last moment," but I keep my mouth shut. Boy am I giving my new mascara the tear test today! I think I will go over to Karen's favorite chocolate shop on Main Street, and share a piece of chocolate with her later today. Karen had a preferred customer card there. It is one of my souvenirs of her life.

Karen would not want me to grieve her. She would be proud of the small ways Ken and I have honored her memory anonymously, such as sending a needy junior-high-school student to church summer camp. She would say, "Don't put store-bought flowers on my grave; give me a wild flower instead as you remember my free spirit now. Help someone less fortunate celebrate their life."

I often feel Karen behind me, just off my shoulders, encouraging me, saying, "Do it, Mom," or "Go for it, Mom," or "You can do it, Mom." She is here with me today as I type this, saying, "Be open and share your heart with others so they can learn and grow through your experiences as you journey down the road to a new and better person." She understands my need for her, but for now we are connected only through the spirit of our love. Some day, in the far off future, we will be together again when the time is right for me to join her.

As I venture down the road of life, I am on the look out for ways that I can honor my daughter. The best way I can do this is to be the best possible person that I can be today as I plan for tomorrow.

The positive things in my life

I could take a bunch of fresh flowers and remove the petals one by one and still have more to say about the positive things in my life.

Ken and I are still married. It has taken a lot of determination and patience to stay together. We have supported each other as we grieved differently and then together. We opened our lines of communication to each other and now talk about our feelings. Our love for each other has changed through this and grown stronger in ways we never imagined.

Pepper lets me know whenever Brian drives in the driveway, and this puts a smile on my face. There is no sweeter word in the world than hearing Brian say "Mom." My love for him grows stronger every day. I want to be here for him and perhaps some day he will make me a grandma.

I have so many new friends who care about me and support me as I go about my life. I don't have to share my past unless I wish to. I still hear, "I don't know how you do it." I often reply, "It is because I choose to remember my daughter, but I now need to live life for me, or it is by the Grace of God".

Life is good. Tomorrow is another day to discover.

I no longer always have to cry when I remember Karen. The memory of her puts a smile on my face today. The years may separate us now, but I am still alive today.

Chapter 10.

The years start to fly by

For a long time, I was stuck in the grief and despair that Karen was gone. People would ask me how long had it been since Karen died. At that time, I thought it would be impossible for the years to fly by. Then, suddenly, I realized one day that the years had flown by.

What made the difference in the way I thought? I said to myself, "Look at me, I am really moving on with my life."

I am living in new and different ways

My grief made me think of myself as if I were a piece of clay or Play Dough. In my grief and pain, I could reshape my life from the raw beginning. I had hit the bottom of the pit. Now, as I re-emerged in life, I had the opportunity to change myself. I could change my hair color, my style of dress and even my weight. I could take the raw piece of clay and reform who I was on the outside. I could totally change my physical appearance. What little flaws did I have that I wanted to get rid of short of plastic surgery?

If I changed my outward appearance, could I then change my mental attitude? Yes, and here again I had choices to make. I could wipe away my tears and only cry on the inside. I could slowly, over time, make small adjustments to improve myself. No, I did not want to look like my grandmother in her 50's and I wanted to shake the image of a woman who did not look after her body. Over time, I began to make some changes as I worked on myself improvement. I decide to form the clay into a flower. Me.

Life is for the living and I want to live

As the new flower began to unfold, I began to look at all the different ways I could and wanted to live my life. I wanted to be in rich soil, so I could grow to be a strong healthy plant. I wanted to replant strong roots in my life so I could weather future storms. I wanted to feel loved and nurtured by my family and friends.

I wanted to live life like never before. I wanted to experience new and different things. I had spent so much time hibernating in my shell, now I wanted to stick my head out again and explore the world.

I surprised Ken and all of my friends when I decided to go on a "girls' trip" to Bali for the fifth anniversary of Karen's death. I took Karen with me in spirit; she would have loved to come with me. One day we visited the Water Palace, and as I walked alone, Karen said to me, "Thanks, Mom, for bringing me here; I am really enjoying the trip."

Over the past few years, I have done so many new and different things that were out of character for the old Jan.

In those days, I was like an old card-catalog boxes in the libraries. Friends use to tell me I was a very compartmentalized person. I opened only one of the catalog boxes at a time. I rarely overlapped things in my life; I was very predictable. Today it could be mahjongg in the morning followed by lunch with friends, and golf as the sun fades over the mountains.

Now, with all the personal growth I was forced to face, I wanted to live life to the fullest, but how? Would Ken go along with me on this one?

I have grown in so many ways

God did not intend for Karen to die. He was just as hurt as I was. Some will say it was for the best that Karen died, or they might say it was part of God's plan for her. I want to scream at them. It was not part of God's plan for her. They are so far from the truth. I have learned compassion for these people.

I have had countless people ask me what the one thing is that I have learned on this journey. My first response is compassion for others and myself. Compassion is a huge word. It has taken me years to fully grasp the realm and complexity of the word. Along with it comes patience.

Compassion begins with me. I had to give myself a break before I could give others the leeway they needed. Today, when someone wants to talk about an experience in their life, I am much more patient as I listen to them. I know that through their talking, they too are letting go and moving forward with their own grief.

Listening, I believe, goes hand in hand with compassion. I had many wonderful people listen to me as I told my story of Karen's death so many times. There is an art to listening. When we listen to the other person with sincerity, we are also helping ourselves perfect our skills. The more I listen, the more I can learn about myself and others.

I have learned how to humble myself in so many ways, like never before. As my mother aged, I learned how to be thoughtful to the elderly. I learned how not to get pushy with her. From my molestation, I learned how to listen as I offered words of encouragement to a young woman who was recently abused.

Through my own growth in grief, I have seen how others have also grown around me. Life is about observation and learning as we encourage each other in life.

I am a much stronger person

The price was too high to pay for this lesson in life. A thousand times, I have wished I had died of cancer and not Karen. We do not have the luxury of getting to choose how and when and of what we will die.

Then one day I woke up and said, "Jan, you can and will be a much stronger person if you listen to your inner self and take the guidance of those around you." From that day forward I decided to read and learn as much as I could about this new journey called grief into which I was suddenly thrust.

I am stronger because I choose to be stronger. I don't want be like the weeping willow in my back yard. I want to stand strong as I face adversity, knowing that sometimes I will fall down or have to bend a little. If I picture myself as a strong person, then it helps me move forward as I learn from my past.

I learned to face my own cancer

It began as one of those small moles we all have; only this one looked different. Somehow, I just knew I had to call my dermatologist. A week or so later, I was in his office and he said, "I don't like the looks of this mole; it has to come off now." Two days later, I was back having it removed, and waiting for the test results.

I was in the waiting room in Donn's office when I called for my test results. Donn walked out to get me as I learned I had melanoma cancer. I was a wreck as I told Donn. Donn again said he would be there for me.

I had always joked that one day I would end up with skin cancer, because of my childhood on San Diego Bay. In those days, we'd never heard of sun block. Now I was going to pay the price, whatever that was. Now the joke had come true. I had to play the wait-and-see game all over again: wait to see the oncologist, then wait to have a larger biopsy taken, and wait again for the test results.

Through all of this, I thought about what Karen must have thought as she waited. She kept so much of her frustration to herself. I drew strength about my own fate with cancer when I thought about how brave Karen had been. If she could do it, so could I. Somehow, I was using reverse mother-daughter support in my mind. Now it was mother who found comfort from her daughter.

We all breathed a huge sigh of relief when the second biopsy showed I was now cancer free. Today, I know the chances of my melanoma reoccurring are strong. I have Ken check my body now for anything unusual. I ask my masseuse to check for new moles too. Most of all, I keep my regularly scheduled doctors appointments.

We cannot avoid the imperfections in life, but we can learn where and how to find the strength to face them. God did not promise us a peaceful rose garden. There will be thorns in life. Now with our new outlook on life, we must decide how we can best face them.

Look out world! I am coming back to life

The rose bud is now starting to bloom. Look out world, here I come. I am the new and improved me. I have learned so much about life in the past six years. Now I want to live life to the fullest.

There have been many days when Ken has just stood back and said, "What?" He shakes his head, and said, "There she goes again."

As I bloom in life and continue to knock my husband off his feet, I do try to do it nicely. Ken is glad to see his old/new wife emerging and full of life now.

I have new hobbies and new interests now

I recently took golf lessons and bought a set of golf clubs. This was a major surprise to Ken and Donn. "Jan is taking up what?" My sense of humor is back now too.

I am in a whole new world of discovery. We have over 325 miles of walking/biking trails in our community, so I got a mountain bike. I'm slowly getting out on the trails.

I recently went horse back riding for the first time in 30 years. I reminded myself that it is a good idea to ask the wrangler to adjust your stirrups when they are too short so your knees don't ache for days when you get off the horse. Life is like this too: sometime we need to stop and make adjustments so our life can run a little easier and we don't have to hobble around.

Laughter is a crucial medicine in coping with grief. The good news is that it does not require a prescription.

Volunteering is a way to give back

My family has always believed in volunteering. Over the years, I have been involved with many organizations. I thought, why not give back some of my talents again? Some of my volunteer work is for a one-time event; sometimes I take on long-term commitments.

One of my most treasured possessions of Karen's is a small poster board and crepe paper cross that she made at Vacation Bible School when she was in fifth grade. It sits on the book case in my office. This past summer, I taught Vacation Bible School with a good friend. Pam and I were the "story hour ladies" to more that 100 children for five days. We dressed in costumes and did silly skits. We had a ball. If one child remembers one thing from one of the lessons we taught them, I accomplished my goal for the week.

Giving back is about letting life come full circle.

I will never forget my daughter

Life is about remembering Karen in a new and healthy way. She will always be a part of me. I will always love her. Karen knows I love her more than life itself, but I must now live my life for me. Today, Karen is up in the grandstands of life cheering me on in whatever I do, saying, "Way to go, Mom."

Karen thanks for the memories! I love each and every one, from our arguments to our celebrations. You were and are my life. You brought me such joy from the moment I knew you were in my womb to seeing you pass into the arms of Jesus. You taught me so much about life, and how to live it.

Abraham Lincoln once said, *"It's not the years in your life that count...It's the life in your years"*. I believe they leave huge footprints in our minds forever. Karen, you were one such person! Thank you for being you!

Life is now worth living for me

Life is also about knowing when it is time for us to move on. There comes a time in our grief when we need to step back away from it and let it slowly drift into the back of our minds. This is moving on in life. No one else can do it for us. We must do it on our own personal timetable.

So how did I know that it is time for me to move on? My inner self was saying it is time.

Remember, there is a huge difference between remembering and reliving. I once met a mother who had lost her daughter at the age of 25 and she was now in her 90's. She told me that every day she remembered her daughter. The years had softened the pain, but her heart still ached to be with her daughter. For over 65 years, this woman had grieved for her daughter every day. Because we loved, we will miss them forever.

I need to celebrate Karen's life by living mine to the maximum each and every day. If the shoe was on the other foot, I would have wanted Karen to continue with her life and live it for herself not me. Now I must do the same.

I find beauty in each new day

I am going to sit outside now, as the sun is setting over the mountains this evening. I will count the blessings that I have had today. For a brief moment, I will remember my past. Most of all I will look forward to the sunrise tomorrow as I welcome a new day.

God Bless…

Epilogue

I hope you have enjoyed reading my book. I never set out to write a "how to book" or any book at all. Never in my wildest dreams pre 2001 did I ever think I would write a book. Then my life was changed forever.

Then I found the need for a book I couldn't find in my local books stores so I decided to venture out of my box and write. I wanted to create a book where we could visit one grieving mother to another. I hope you curled up in your favorite chair with the beverage of your choice as you read my story. I kept it short so you could read it in a couple of hours. I wanted to show you through my examples how I found hope, and found comfort in the darkest of days.

Yes, there are days when I still miss Karen beyond words, I always will shed a tear now and then, or create my own flash flood of tears. Just because she died I haven't stopped being her mother. Just as I know you will never stop being the mother of your child. Therefore we will all cry from time to time.

If I have helped ease or showed you another way to look at your grief, then I have accomplished my goal in sharing my story with you.

I would like to thank all of my friends who encouraged me to write this book. There were days and weeks when I was so unsure of myself. All of these wonderful friends helped keep me focused on creating my book. They all knew someone who could have benefited from a book like mine.

I took a class one summer at Salt Lake Theological Seminary on the Book of Ruth. I can associate with Naomi over the death of her sons. I know her pain. I can relate to Orpah when she decides against following Naomi and Ruth. It is sometimes easier to stay in my comfort zone. I am like Ruth when she realizes she must move on with her life. I too have had to begin a new life and move forward. Each of these women gives me strength.

Today, I am a member of the Park City Community Church, a United Methodist Church. The sanctuary is surrounded by wonderful windows that look out to God's creation the mountains. Have you ever had a moose upstage the pastor on this hill behind the pulpit as he gave the sermon? Ken often attends church with me, but he is still a Lutheran at heart.

Ken recently retired. We embarked on another new journey in lives. Ken at long last has the time he has longed for to pursue his long forgotten hobbies. Together the chapters of our lives just continue to grow.

Ken and I just took a short trip with friends in our sports cars to southern Utah. I have never laughed so much. There is so much to be grateful in this world. I just marveled at the diversity of the landscape. It is so beautiful. There is still so much of this world I want to see and to learn about. I know God isn't done with me yet!

I am learning to live, laugh and love again, each day. I am available to travel and share my story of hope. I am sure we can find something to laugh about too as we continue to learn.

I can be reached at jansbook@mwutah.com.

Printed in the United States
92120LV00006B/13-33/A